& poo

From Good to Better

A Quality Improvement Audit for all Childcare Providers

REDCAR & CLEVELAND
BOROUGH COUNCIL

Early Years Support Team
Proud to be learning together

Published 2009 by A & C Black Publishers Limited
36 Soho Square, London W1D 3QY
www.acblack.com

ISBN 978-1-4081-1252-6

Text © Redcar and Cleveland Council, 2009

A CIP record for this publication is available from the British Library.

Printed in Great Britain by Martins the Printers, Berwick-on-Tweed

This book is produced using paper that is made from wood grown in managed, sustainable forests. It is natural, renewable and recyclable. The logging and manufacturing processes conform to the environmental regulations of the country of origin.

To see our full range of titles
visit www.acblack.com

Contents

Introduction

The *Early Years Support Team* in Redcar and Cleveland has developed this book in response to a frequent and important question from their practitioners: 'How do we turn an Ofsted judgement from good into outstanding?' Using this audit tool will help settings identify where they are now and enable them to plan for improvement. It is designed to help practitioners complete the *Ofsted Self Evaluation Form* and to collect and record relevant evidence as part of the process of continuous assessment and self-evaluation.

The Childcare Act (2006) places a requirement on Local Authorities to provide sufficient childcare to enable parents and carers to work, but also to ensure that the childcare provision is of a high quality. *The National Quality and Improvement Network* (NQIN) states that:

> 'Local authorities and national organisations ensure quality improvement is achievable, continuous and sustainable.' *(NQIN Principle 11)*

The Redcar and Cleveland team believe that achieving quality is a journey and not a destination and that quality improvement should be an on-going and evolving process. This book will help local authorities to meet *Principle 11* and to work towards implementing a further NQIN Principle:

> 'Local authorities and national organisations monitor quality improvements and communicate achievements.' *(NQIN Principle 10)*

The overall aim of this book is not just to improve the quality or provision in Redcar and Cleveland but for children and families everywhere.

How to use this book

This book can be used in a variety of ways, with early years settings, practitioners and childminders. It is designed so that one part can be used as an individual focus, more than one part can be used in a combination or it can be used as a whole. A setting could, for example, focus on raising one outcome from satisfactory to good or it could choose to improve all outcomes.

We would recommend that settings or practitioners initially use the audit on all five outcomes to gather an overall picture. The audit page can be photocopied and a highlighter pen can be used to assess where the settings or practitioners feel they are now. This should be dated and used as evidence for the 'Ofsted Self Evaluation Form'. Any relevant evidence should be collected at this point. The settings or practitioners could then choose to focus on all or a number of outcomes. An action plan, which has a timescale and people identified, can then be drawn up and implemented. This establishes a process of continuous development.

The sections on the audit, what will happen during the Ofsted inspection, policies and documentation and examples of good practice within this book need to be put into context for individual practitioners.

Local Authorities can support settings or practitioners through this process, 'encouraging settings to innovate through self evaluation' (NQIN Principles). In Redcar and Cleveland we use the audit to establish a baseline for our settings or practitioners and as a tool to measure improvement.

This book provides a common language for settings, practitioners and Local Authorities to use when sharing good practice or discussing practice issues, and would provide a focus for networking groups.

Be Healthy

	Outstanding	Good	Satisfactory	Inadequate 1	Inadequate 2
Practitioners follow appropriate policies	Policies and procedures in place and strictly adhered to by practitioners, parents and students. Confident practitioners are proud of their high standards of cleanliness and are proactive in maintaining them. All practitioners are trained in paediatric first aid. Babies have own creams, etc. for nappy changing. All practitioners keep accident and medicine books up to date and ensure parents have signed them.	Policies and procedures in place and promoted by all practitioners and students. All practitioners are proactive about cleanliness. All practitioners are trained in paediatric first aid. Practitioners personalise nappy changing time. Accident and medicine books are completed and kept up to date and signed by parents.	Policies in place and reviewed. Procedures understood by practitioners. Setting is clean at the beginning of the day and surfaces are wiped during the day. All practitioners are trained in paediatric first aid. Nappy changing routines are followed. Accident and medicine books are completed.	Policies in place, but not read by all practitioners. Procedures not followed by all. Setting unclean, surface cleaning inconsistent. Some practitioners are trained in paediatric first aid. Protective clothing not worn during nappy changing. Accident and medicine books are not complete.	Policies not in place. Procedures not clear and not followed. Setting unclean. Cleaning not carried out during the day. Some practitioners trained in paediatric first aid. Protective clothing not available to wear during nappy changing. Accident and medicine books are missing or incomplete.
Children understand simple good health/ hygiene practices	Children wash their hands independently at appropriate times. They encourage and support each other and fully understand the importance of their own personal hygiene. Wash and toilet areas are clean and personalised with children's own flannel, towel and toothbrush, which are regularly washed. Children are encouraged to brush their teeth after lunch.	Children wash their hands at appropriate times. Children understand the importance of personal hygiene. Toilet areas are pleasant and children use the wet flannels provided by the practitioner. Most children have their own toothbrush and brush their teeth after lunch.	Children are told to wash their hands at appropriate times. Children have some understanding of the importance of personal hygiene. Toilet areas are clean at start of day and practitioners wipe children's hands and faces.	Children are not encouraged to wash their hands. Children have limited understanding of the importance of personal hygiene. Toilet areas are not clean and inadequately stocked. Children's hands and faces are rarely washed.	Practitioners do not mention hand washing. Children have no understanding of the importance of personal hygiene. Toilet areas are dirty and there are insufficient supplies of toilet paper and paper towels.

	Outstanding	Good	Satisfactory	Inadequate 1	Inadequate 2
Children are nourished	Children eat varied, well-balanced meals and snacks. The setting consults with parents on special dietary needs (including religious) and welcomes suggestions for meals. Most food is organic. Food from other cultures is included. Wide choice of drinks, snacks and meals are offered to children.	Children eat well-balanced meals and snacks. Parents are consulted on dietary needs on admission and can view menu. Some food is organic. Some foods from different cultures are included. Children are offered a choice of drinks and snacks.	Most meals are well-balanced. The setting is informed by parents about dietary needs. Some food is cooked on site. Some fresh and some processed food is used. Foods from other cultures are introduced. Children are offered limited choices of meals, snacks and drinks.	Little regard is paid to well-balanced meals. Practitioners do not always know children's dietary needs. Little food is prepared from fresh and most food is processed. Children occasionally given food from other cultures. Children offered no choice of meals, snacks and drinks.	No regard is paid to well-balanced meals. Children's dietary needs are ignored, putting children in danger. All food is processed. Children not given the opportunity to try foods from other cultures. Children served with meals and drinks but snacks are not offered.
Children enjoy physical activity	A wide range of exciting and challenging outdoor and indoor quality play equipment and ample space is always available. Children have free access to outdoor areas. All practitioners always participate with the children to encourage and support them in physical activities.	A range of indoor and outdoor equipment and sufficient space is always available. Activities present some challenge. Children have some free access to outdoors. Most practitioners participate with the children to encourage them in physical activities.	A limited range of indoor and outdoor equipment and space is available. Activities present little challenge. Access to outdoor activities is timetabled. Some practitioners participate with the children in physical activities.	Little indoor and outdoor equipment and space is available. Activities present no challenge. Children are only allowed outside for short periods of time. Practitioners rarely participate with the children in physical activities.	Inappropriate indoor and outdoor equipment is available. Children rarely go outside. Practitioners never participate with the children in physical activities.
Learn about healthy living	Children have a solid understanding about healthy eating and exercise. They understand the effects of exercise on their body and that they need to drink water which they can access independently.	Children understand about healthy eating and exercise. They understand that exercise affects their body. They know that they need to drink water regularly and it is readily available.	Children have some understanding of healthy eating and exercise. They know about some of the effects of exercise on their body. They know they need to drink water, which is available all the time.	Children have limited understanding of healthy eating and exercise. They do not understand about the effects of exercise on their body. Practitioners serve water sometimes.	Children have no understanding of healthy eating and exercise. They do not understand about the effects that exercise has on their body. Water is not available.
Rest and sleep according to their needs	Routines are flexible and all children can rest or sleep when they need to. They have their own pillows and blanket. Cosy, draped sleeping areas are set up in all rooms. Practitioners are sensitive to the children's needs.	Routines allow for most children to sleep when they need to. There are comfortable areas set up where the children can rest or sleep. Practitioners show care towards tired children.	Routines fit around some children's needs. There are some cosy areas set up where children can rest or sleep. Practitioners show some care towards tired children.	Routines are rigid with little regard for children's need to rest or sleep. The sleeping area is not attractive and inviting. Practitioners show little care towards tired children.	There are set sleep times. No regard for individual children's needs. Quiet areas where children can nap not set up. Practitioners show no care towards tired children.

What will happen during the Ofsted inspection?

What will the inspector expect to see?	What might the inspector ask?	What can I do to prepare?
• A high standard of cleanliness • Daily routines for maintaining cleaning standards • COSHH information/booklets • Separate ancillary staff	• Where are cleaning products stored? • What training have you undertaken with regard to COSHH?	• Promote high standards of cleanliness • Ensure practitioners balance the need for a child to finish eating/activity before cleaning surfaces • Ensure the safe storage of cleaning fluids • Ensure cleaning time is separate from play time
• Good systems in place for personal hygiene • Nappy changing routine displayed • Photographs that demonstrate hand washing for older children • A procedure for the protection of children with regard to pets	• Do the children have their own flannels, towels, nappy cream, etc? • How do you avoid cross infection at nappy changing?	• Ensure that all practitioner's understand nappy changing routine • Keep toilet areas/nappy changing areas well stocked • Highlight the importance of personal hygiene
• Practitioners who know what to do when a child is ill or has an accident • Communicable diseases information for practitioners and parents • A sign for parents indicating name of appointed first aider • RIDDOR information	• What do you do if a child becomes ill? • What do you do if a child has an accident? • What do you need to do if a parent asks you to give medicine? • How would you report a serious accident and to whom?	• Ensure that all practitioners understand relevant policies • Provide relevant documentation • Ensure that the First Aid box is always stocked and products are not out of date • Ensure practitioners are aware of their roles with regard to first aid
• Well-balanced meals, with opportunities for children to develop independence • Individual needs met i.e. special diets	• Can I see today's/this week's menus? • Is water available for children to access all day?	• Devise nutritious, balanced menus, including snacks • Ensure that drinking water is available at all times • Provide table cloths/table mats • Make sure age appropriate utensils are available

Be Healthy

Policies and documentation

Policies

- Health and safety
- Food and drink
- Medication
- Allergies
- Care, learning and play
- Health, illness and emergency
- No smoking

Documentation

- Accident records, including practitioner and parent signatures
- Medication treatment records, including practitioner and parent signatures
- Form for consent to take child to hospital
- Records of practitioner first aid training
- Menus
- Records of Food Hygiene training
- Children's contact and permission details for all outings

Other resources

- Well stocked and up to date First Aid box
- Smaller First Aid boxes to take on outings and in all transport

Examples of good practice
Practitioners follow appropriate policies

Examples of good practice

All appropriate policies and procedures are in place and are part of an induction programme for new members of staff. The setting is fresh and clean at the beginning of the day and practitioners are proactive in maintaining cleanliness during the day. Practitioners are sensitive to children's interests and do not interrupt children's activities to wipe surfaces. All practitioners have emergency First Aid, and all have paediatric first aid.

Practitioners make nappy changing time special by talking to the babies. Practitioners have a responsibility towards keeping the accident and medicine book up to date, keeping parents informed of any incidents and requesting signatures where necessary.

Nappy disposal units are emptied on a regular basis. All bins have lids and are emptied throughout the day.

From good to better

All policies and procedures are in place and are part of a comprehensive induction and ongoing training programme for practitioners and students. All practitioners are proud of their standards of cleanliness and are proactive about maintaining them. Children understand why cleanliness is important and join in with appropriate activities. All practitioners have paediatric first aid and are committed to further training.

All practitioners make nappy changing time personal by engaging with babies and young children and taking their time. Babies have their own cream.

Separate ancillary staff are employed at the beginning and end of the day to clean the setting and make sure it is stocked appropriately.

Examples of good practice

Children understand simple good health/hygiene practices

Examples of good practice

Practitioners praise children for washing their hands and discuss with them why it is important. Toilet areas are pleasantly decorated and practitioners check during the day that they are well stocked and have no unpleasant odours.

Children are beginning to understand why it is important to brush their teeth after meals.

From good to better

Children confidently wash their hands before snack and meal times. They remind each other if someone forgets. Wash areas are welcoming and clean and smell pleasantly of air freshener. Children have their own towels, flannels, and toothbrushes. Children access these independently.

Children brush their teeth after lunch and dental hygienists are invited into the setting to help the children understand the importance of looking after their teeth.

Examples of good practice

Children are well nourished

Examples of good practice

Children eat a nutritious and balanced diet. Some food is organic. Fresh fruit and vegetables are given for snacks and included in most meals when possible. Babies who are being weaned are introduced to fresh fruit and vegetables in a suitable form. Meals and snack times are planned around their routines.

Fresh drinking water is available at all times in cups or bottles. Where appropriate children are able to access this themselves. Foods from other cultures are introduced as part of the main menu e.g. Chinese food as part of Chinese New Year celebrations.

Parents are asked if children have any food allergies, dietary requirements, likes or dislikes on admission. Children choose whether they want milk or water and pour it for themselves. Practitioners encourage the children to try different foods.

From good to better

Children eat a wholesome, nutritious and well-balanced diet.

Meals are freshly prepared using fresh fruit and vegetables, some using organic or homegrown produce. Foods from other cultures and religions are included in meals and snacks. The children are able to grow some of their own food. They are often involved in helping to prepare their own meals by picking vegetables from the garden and preparing them.

Parents are regularly consulted about dietary requirements and preferences. Menus are produced to give parents information about choices.

Children are given excellent choices about the drinks and snacks they would like and serve themselves and each other at the table at meal times. The tables are set attractively, with each child having their own place mat and cutlery. Practitioners develop meal times as a social occasion.

Examples of good practice
Children enjoy physical activity

Examples of good practice

Babies and children are encouraged in physical play. Room layout takes into consideration the changing needs of babies when they start to become mobile. Inside there is home-style furniture that babies beginning to walk can hold on to.

All children, including babies, have some access to the outdoors every day. Outside there is sufficient space for children to run, roll, crawl, climb, explore and build with a range of equipment. Children are offered opportunities to dance to music or meet the challenge of an obstacle course. Practitioners support and encourage the children in their physical play by waiting to catch them at the bottom of the slide or joining in with running races.

From good to better

Babies and children are encouraged to participate in robust physical exercise. They use the outdoor facilities, including a climbing frame and slide, with gusto and have good control over their bodies.

There is a good variety of climbing frames, suitable for all age groups, which children use in an imaginative way, one day a fire engine, the next an island. Children have free access to the outside area. Suitable clothing and footwear are provided for wet weather. Older children are encouraged to dress themselves for outdoors. Practitioners make good use of the surrounding area with visits to the park, woodland or beach.

Practitioners are aware of the need to provide 'safe' challenges, e.g. increasing the height of equipment for some children, while supporting others.

Practitioners use a variety of music for children to move to, including classical. They note the likes of very young children and respond. Practitioners enthusiastically join in with free movement.

They share in the fun and become part of the games.

A dance teacher comes in on a weekly basis.

Examples of good practice
Children learn about healthy living

Examples of good practice

Children take part in a topic about healthy eating. They learn about the need to eat five portions of fruit and vegetables a day. They begin to be able to name some fruit and some vegetables. They help to grow some fruit/vegetables outdoors, observing changes and harvesting the crop. They use them to make meals or snacks. Sometimes they go to the shops to buy ingredients.

They are presented with some food in different forms e.g. boiled potatoes and jacket potatoes and practitioners talk about the changes that have occurred.

All children are presented with healthy snack choices and even young children are encouraged to make choices.

Practitioners encourage children to run around, jump up and down and then talk about the changes in their body, asking questions like "Can you feel your heart beating really fast?", "Does your face look red and feel hot?", "How can we cool ourselves down?" The children understand that they will need to drink water and it is readily available.

From good to better

Children have weekly cooking activities and make simple healthy snacks e.g. putting healthy toppings on pizzas, making pictures with fresh vegetables. The activities are fun, stimulating and emphasise the importance of healthy food such as fresh fruit and vegetables.

Children understand the effects of exercise on their bodies and remark that they are out of breath because they have been running really fast.

Examples of good practice
Rest and sleep according to their needs

Examples of good practice

Cosy areas are available for all children with cushions, beanbags and drapes if appropriate. The practitioner acknowledges that a child is tired and picks them up and sits in a quiet area, affectionately cuddling the child until he/she falls asleep. The practitioner then takes the child to the rest area and lays her/him down, covering her/him with a blanket.

Parents are informed on a daily basis about their child's day including feeding and sleeping.

From good to better

Lighting can be dimmed in the cosy area. A child falls asleep on a cushion in the book area. The practitioner leaves the child there, covers him with a blanket and encourages other children playing nearby to move their play to another area in the room.

Stay Safe

Audit

	Outstanding	Good	Satisfactory	Inadequate 1	Inadequate 2
Premises are safe, secure and suitable for their purpose. Adequate space is offered in appropriate location	High levels of safety and security are adhered to. Robust procedures are in place for visitors. Practitioners check premises daily, indoor and out, to ensure they are clean, safe and secure. There is space for children to play, eat and rest. Toilets and nappy changing areas are clearly defined. Practitioners have access to a private, comfortable area for breaks. Kitchen and laundry facilities are available. Safe and accessible storage cupboards. Highly effective systems are in place for children to arrive and leave setting.	Effective levels of safety and security are adhered to. Effective procedures are in place for visitors. Practitioners check indoor and outdoor premises regularly. Space is well organised for children to play, eat and rest. Toilets and nappy changing areas are in appropriate spaces. Practitioners have access to a comfortable area for breaks. Kitchen and some laundry facilities are available. Safe storage areas are available. Effective systems are in place for children to arrive and leave setting.	Premises are secure and safe. Visitors sign in on entry. Practitioners check indoor and outdoor premises for safety but not consistently. Space is organised to meet the needs of most children. Toilets and nappy changing areas are appropriate. Small staff room housing a washing machine and small kitchen. Storage space is available in some areas. Children arrive and leave setting safely.	Appropriate steps have been taken to ensure premises are safe but not always consistent. Procedures for visitors not followed. Space is not well organised to accommodate children's daily routine activities. Nappy changing area inappropriately placed. Cluttered staff room. Kitchen is inappropriately equipped. Poor laundry facilities. Little or no storage areas. Children arrive and leave setting with inappropriate safety procedures.	Steps to maintain appropriate levels of security are not followed. No procedures for visitors. Space is not clearly defined in order for children to follow their daily routines. Play space restricted due to fixed space for snacks and meal times. Nappy changing area is not suitable. Toilets lack privacy. No area for staff breaks. Kitchen unsafe. No laundry facilities. No storage. Random toys stored untidily. More supervision required when children arrive and leave setting.
Premises are welcoming to children and offer access to the necessary facilities for a range of activities which promote their development	All areas of the setting are warm, welcoming and inviting. The setting is light and well ventilated with a high standard of décor. Well-planned areas to meet all children's needs. External safety agencies are regularly used to support children's understanding of safety.	Setting is mainly warm, welcoming and inviting. The setting is light and well ventilated with appropriate décor. Areas are planned to meet most children's needs. External safety agencies are used to support children's understanding of safety.	Setting is warm with some areas inviting. Some areas well lit and ventilated. Some areas appropriately decorated. Appropriately planned areas to meet children's needs. Activities incorporate some safety themes.	Some areas are inviting but some lack warmth. Some areas are dark with little ventilation. Décor is in need of attention. Inappropriate planning, space is cluttered and children's needs not met. Children have little awareness of outside safety agencies.	Areas lack warmth and don't feel welcoming and inviting. No natural light, no ventilation. Decorating in poor repair. No planning, Space cluttered. Environment detrimental to children's needs. Children have no awareness of outside safety agencies.

From Good to Better © Redcar & Cleveland 2009

	Outstanding	Good	Satisfactory	Inadequate 1	Inadequate 2
Furniture, equipment and toys are appropriate for purpose and create an accessible and stimulating environment	Furniture, equipment and toys are stage appropriate and meet the needs of all children in the setting. Excellent range of resources placed to allow safe and independent access. A multi-cultural society is reflected within the resources Evidence of equal opportunities in play. Environment vibrant for all age groups.	Furniture, equipment and toys are fit for purpose and meet the needs of the children. They are interesting and independently accessible. Some resources reflect multi-cultural society. Evidence of equal opportunities in play. Environment exciting and stimulating for all age groups.	Most furniture, equipment and toys appropriate for age range and accessible for children. Few resources reflect multi-cultural society. Some evidence of equal opportunities in play. Some elements of environment stimulating.	Some furniture, equipment and toys appropriate for purpose but children can only access some themselves. Some resources are unsuitable. Little evidence of resources which reflect multi-cultural society. Environment lacks interest and excitement.	Furniture inappropriate size. Equipment and toys not organised between rooms to be stage appropriate. Resources inappropriate and children not encouraged to access them independently. No evidence of resources which reflect multi-cultural society. Environment lacks interest.
Furniture, equipment and toys are of suitable design and condition, well maintained and conform to safety standards	All furniture, equipment and toys conform to the highest standards of exceptional quality. All in immaculate condition through routine rigorous checking and cleaning by practitioners. Detailed inventory of play equipment regularly updated.	Furniture, equipment and toys conform to high standards of quality. Resources in quality condition due to regular checking and cleaning by practitioners. Inventory of play equipment in place.	Furniture equipment and toys conform to a reasonable standard. Practitioners check condition and clean resources but not on a regular basis. Record of some resources provided in setting.	Furniture equipment and toys are in poor condition. Little evidence of checking and cleaning of resources. No evidence of record of resources in setting.	Furniture equipment and toys are inappropriate. No evidence of checking and cleaning of resources. No record kept of resources.
Practitioners promote safety within the setting and on outings. Precautions are taken against accidents	Excellent health and safety policies and procedures. All practitioners consulted when policies being reviewed. Very conscientious practitioners demonstrate a solid understanding of them. A designated practitioner has responsibility for health and safety. Thorough risk assessments carried out daily. Robust procedures in place for outings. Parents and visitors are encouraged to be vigilant. Practitioners consistently encourage children to be safety minded. Health and safety records maintained and up to date.	Effective health and safety policies and procedures in place. Senior practitioners consulted when policies are being reviewed and practitioners show a clear understanding of them. A designated practitioner has responsibility for health and safety. Risk assessments are an ongoing process. Effective procedures in place for outings. Parents and visitors are invited to identify hazards and concerns. Practitioners encourage the children to be safety minded. Health and safety records maintained.	Manager ensures health and safety policies in place. All practitioners have an awareness of them. A designated practitioner has responsibility for health and safety but not all practitioners aware of this. Risk assessments carried out as and when necessary. Appropriate procedures in place for outings. Parents and visitors encouraged to be safety aware as are the children. Practitioners sometimes encourage children to be safety minded. Health and safety records kept.	Health and safety policies insufficient. Practitioners lacking in awareness of them. Some checks are carried out on some elements of safety. No risk assessments in place in setting or on outings. Parents and children are not encouraged to consider safety. Practitioners rarely encourage children to be safety minded. Some health and safety records kept.	No health and safety policies. Practitioners demonstrate little or no knowledge of how to implement them. No safety checks carried out. No risk assessments in evidence in setting and on outings and no understanding of risks and hazards. Parents and children show no regard for the safety of others or of themselves. Practitioners never encourage children to be safety minded. No evidence of health and safety records.

	Outstanding	Good	Satisfactory	Inadequate 1	Inadequate 2
Registered person complies with local safeguarding children procedures, approved by LSB and ensures all adults looking after the children are able to put the procedures into practice	Clear policies and robust procedures in place and understood by all practitioners and parents. All practitioners consulted when policies being reviewed. Practitioners are vigilant and have excellent understanding of how to put procedures into practice. Designated practitioner responsible for liaising with safeguarding children agencies. All practitioners fully trained in the safeguarding of children. Children's records are thorough and up to date.	Effective policies and procedures in place and understood and followed by all practitioners. Senior practitioners consulted when policies being reviewed. Practitioners show real concern and care and are consistent in their implementation of procedures. Designated practitioner trained in the safe-guarding of children and responsible for liaising with safeguarding children agencies. Other practitioners have awareness of safeguarding children training. Children's records are detailed.	Appropriate policies and procedures in place. Most practitioners show an understanding of policies and procedures. Most practitioners show care and concern and know how to implement them in practice. Designated practitioner trained and responsible for safeguarding children. Children's records are appropriate.	Policies and procedures insufficient. Practitioners only have a basic understanding of safeguarding children policies and procedures. They have insufficient understanding of how to implement them. No designated practitioner with responsibility for safeguarding children. Safeguarding children training out of date. Children's records inconsistent.	Policies and procedures inappropriate. Practitioners have little or no understanding of safeguarding children policies and procedures. No designated person with responsibility for safeguarding children. No practitioners have received safeguarding children training. Little evidence of children's records.

From Good to Better © Redcar & Cleveland 2009

What will happen during the Ofsted inspection?

What will the inspector expect to see?	What might the inspector ask?	What can I do to prepare?
• Secure entrance with appropriate safety mechanisms • Signing in and out book • Clean, safe and well maintained environment and equipment • Sufficient areas for storage • Practitioner and child registers	• What would you do if an unidentified person came to collect a child? • Who is responsible for the daily cleaning and checking of the equipment?	• Have clear procedures for collection of children • Ensure all cleaning records/rotas are up to date • Ensure practitioners are aware of their roles and responsibilities
• Warm and welcoming environment • Space, which is organised for children to explore or rest if they wish	• What procedures do you follow with regard to sleeping children? • Who is responsible for the organisation of the rooms?	• Carry out a pre-Ofsted audit on each room • Re-visit children's information with regard to their individual sleeping patterns
• Resources, which are easily accessible, interesting and challenging • Toys, equipment and furniture, which are in good condition • Comfortable area for children to lie down or rest	• What would you do if you found a broken toy? • Who is responsible for the buying/replacement of equipment and how often is this reviewed?	• Have a designated practitioner responsible for safeguarding children • Have areas available for children to sleep when they wish to • Have clear procedures in place for replacing / buying equipment
• Vigilant practitioners regarding children's safety both indoors and outdoors • Practitioners deployed effectively on outings • A regular review of safety arrangements and risk assessments	• How do you ensure the outdoor play space is safe? • How would you undertake a risk assessment for an outing? • When would you undertake a risk assessment? Who would take responsibility for doing this?	• Ensure that a risk assessment is completed each morning prior to children using the area • Have information on all outings, to include risk assessment/ratios, kept in a clearly identified file • Ensure all fire exits are clear from obstruction
• Appointed person responsible for safeguarding children • Arrangements in place for sharing information with parents and relevant agencies	• Who is the responsible person for safeguarding children and what training have they undertaken? • How do you keep up to date with changes in legislation? E.g. which agencies do you liaise with?	• Ensure all practitioners have undertaken training in safe guarding children • Ensure that the nominated person regularly checks the safeguarding children's website should there be any changes in legislation

Policies and documentation

Policies

- Health and safety
- Safeguarding children including procedures for allegations made against a practitioner
- Accident policy
- Medication policy
- Broken toy/equipment policy

Documentation

- Fire drills
- Risk assessment
- Practitioners and children signing in and out records
- Cleaning records/rota
- Sleeping babies monitoring records
- PAT records

Other resources

- Access to a telephone
- Safety equipment e.g. fire blanket, extinguishers
- Locked cabinet for confidential information
- First Aid equipment

Examples of good practice

Premises are safe, secure and suitable for their purpose. Adequate space is offered in appropriate location

Examples of good practice

The entrance has a coded system with a bell tone to alert practitioners. Specific family members and carers are given their own password to gain entry. Visitors are asked to sign the visitor's book and show their identity. The identity of a visitor from the local authority is checked. A childminder's front and back door would be locked at all times. Keys would be taken out of the lock and out of children's reach but accessible to adults.

Low fences surround all outside areas. The fences are in good repair and drains are covered. Gates are bolted.

A practitioner checks the indoor and outdoor premises every morning following a checklist.

Space is suitably defined within each room for children to play, eat and rest. The nappy changing area is separate from the eating area.

Practitioners have a clean, tidy, comfortable area for their breaks. Laundry facilities are separate from the kitchen area. There is a labelled COSHH cupboard and all products are appropriately stored and locked.

There are clear procedures to ensure only authorised people collect children. A grandparent was introduced to a key person as she was going to be collecting the child from the setting later.

From good to better

A biometric system is installed on entrances and exits to ensure that only parents and practitioners whose fingerprints are registered on the system can gain access to the nursery. Parents registered with the nursery can enter and leave while practitioners continue to concentrate on caring for the children.

Well-maintained six foot fences surround all outdoor areas. Gates are high with bolts out of the reach of the children.

A designated practitioner uses a documented checklist when checking premises. The manager actively monitors the checklist and acknowledges that a fire exit has been blocked with equipment. The manager speaks to the staff in the room about this.

The setting has a separate dining room set out with low dining tables, chairs and home-like storage cupboards. There is a home-like area where children can relax at breakfast and after school times. There is a cosy sleeping area that children can go to for a rest when they want.

The staff room is private with kitchen facilities, cloakroom area and personal lockers. There is a well-equipped laundry room with a tumble dryer and efficient ventilation.

There is a clearly identified COSHH cupboard and all other products are stored in well-labelled cupboards out of reach of the children. The biometric system supports the safe arrival and departure of children.

Examples of good practice

Premises are welcoming to children and offer access to the necessary facilities for a range of activities which promote their development

Examples of good practice

The entrance area is clean, light and warm. Most rooms are clean, light and airy with some natural light. There is a welcoming display of pictures of practitioners with their key children in the entrance area. The setting is decorated in calming neutral colours.

The baby room is homely with rugs, cushions and soft drapes. A practitioner is feeding a baby on the sofa. A baby is pulling itself up on a low platform. Babies are sitting in the sand on the floor exploring the texture with their bare toes. A plastic sheet is put down on the floor for children to paint.

Most furniture is age and stage appropriate and promotes children's independence. Most storage is low level and accessible to children.

A childminder would organise their indoor and outdoor space according to the age, stage and interests of their children as appropriate. Where possible low level cupboards and storage boxes would be accessible.

Children have free flow access to outdoors. There is a playhouse and garden area. There is a storage shed and children help practitioners to carry out equipment and tidy it away. Photos of children are attached to the fence.

From good to better

The entrance area is clean, spacious, warm and tidy with a sofa. All rooms are clean and bright with lots of windows with blinds where required. There is a pleasant smell of air freshener throughout and fresh flowers are displayed.

The displays are fresh, attractive and informative. Photo albums are on display in the entrance area, which indicate that displays are child centred and regularly reviewed and updated. There is an alcove for pushchairs.

All rooms are decorated to a high standard and cleanliness is consistently maintained through a cleaning rota and separate ancillary staff.

All areas are well planned and organised and children move freely and safely from one area to another. There is a separate dining room and a large cloakroom area where the pre-school children wash their hands with independence. They said they had to wash germs from their hands before they had their snack.

Adults plan activities for children to learn safety awareness. Local community police officers and fire safety officers come to visit the setting to develop the children's understanding of safety. A return visit to the local fire station is planned.

Examples of good practice

Furniture, equipment and toys are appropriate for purpose and create an accessible and stimulating environment

Examples of good practice

Most furniture is low level in the baby room. It is sturdy and a baby is pulling herself up on the sofa. Furniture is arranged in an attractive way with textured rugs and some natural materials, which babies explore excitedly and independently. All resources are accessible in baskets stored on low level shelves or on the floor.

The pre-school room is defined with wooden screens and some open trellis partitions. All children concentrate on tasks without being distracted by other children who are working nearby. Equipment and resources are stored on surfaces and shelving that the children can access independently. Children are engaged in the sand area building a den for their dinosaurs using twigs, shells and stones. One child sweeps up sand that spilled on to the floor with a hand brush and shovel, which he knew where to find without asking a practitioner.

The role play area is turned into a Chinese restaurant. The practitioner models how to order from one of the menus. Children have lots of choice. Attention is given to meeting all the children's needs. Every part of the setting accessed by the children is eye catching and interesting. All experiences are captured on camera and displayed on the wall.

From good to better

All furniture in all rooms is age and stage appropriate. All rooms have sofas and comfy chairs. Rooms feel cosy and homely due to the clever arrangement of rugs, cushions, plants, interesting everyday objects, natural materials and drapes where appropriate. All resources are sorted into woven baskets of all shapes and sizes, which children can access independently.

Role-play furniture replicates a child's home with kitchen appliances, small clotheshorse, wash basket, dining table, chairs and a high chair. It includes real food packets, tins and baby care products.

Children are engaged with empathy dolls of various nationalities. The children know the names and a three year old talks about the African doll that doesn't have a home like hers but lives in a hut. The environment throughout the setting is eye-catching with textured walls and rugs. Mobiles of photos, everyday objects or children's work hang in all areas. Photos are annotated and displayed where children can see them.

Examples of good practice
Furniture, equipment and toys are of suitable design and condition, well maintained and conform to safety standards

Examples of good practice

Toys, furniture and equipment conform to British Standards Kite mark. Furniture, equipment and toys are in good condition and are checked by staff as they work with the children. A child alerts a practitioner to a plastic vehicle, which is cracked. A discussion develops between them and the child points out that it might be sharp where it is cracked and it is not safe to play with. The practitioner agrees and it is thrown away. All practitioners take responsibility for cleaning toys. An inventory is in place of play equipment.

From good to better

Detailed checklists are kept in each room for checking the condition of toys and the cleaning of them. Practitioners work on a rota and sign the checklist when the checking or cleaning have been their responsibility. A detailed inventory of all furniture, equipment and toys is kept updated.

Examples of good practice

Practitioners promote safety within the setting and on outings. Precautions are taken against accidents

Examples of good practice

All health and safety policies and procedures are in place. Senior practitioners are consulted when policies are being reviewed. A designated practitioner has responsibility for health and safety and is fully trained. Practitioners gain support by working alongside more experienced colleagues. Practitioners demonstrate their understanding by anticipating and preventing accidents. A practitioner notices children stacking building crates too high and intervenes to ensure children's safety.

Risk assessments are made daily. Outings are planned and risk assessments carried out. Children going on a walk to the park are engaged in a discussion with the practitioner about walking sensibly along by the roadside with their partner to keep safe from cars.

All practitioners attend paediatric first aid training.

From good to better

All health and safety policies and procedures are in place. All practitioners are consulted when policies are up for renewal. A designated practitioner has responsibility for health and safety and is fully trained. Practitioners are well qualified and knowledgeable. Effective induction and ongoing training, with regular monitoring and support, ensure that practitioners understand and follow procedures to keep children safe. Children take increasing responsibility for their own safety, through clear support and positive encouragement from practitioners.

Risk assessments are made of all areas within the setting and reviewed by the designated practitioner for health and safety. All practitioners are made aware of possible risks and informed of the positive action they must take to prevent accidents. All outings are well planned. Practitioners make visits before they take children to the venues and liaise with the owners to make a full risk assessment. Children are informed in advance of outings to help them understand how they must behave to stay safe, e.g. holding hands when walking along the road.

Parents participate in keeping the children safe when they attend the nursery by adhering to nursery policies. Children stay safe because their concerns are taken seriously. Children enjoy sliding down a fire fighter's pole with practitioners nearby to catch them if necessary, but are not over protected. Records are thorough and up to date.

Examples of good practice

Registered person complies with local safeguarding children procedures approved by LSB and ensures all adults are able to put the procedures into practice.

Examples of good practice

All safeguarding children policies and procedures are in place. Room leaders are consulted when policies need renewing. All practitioners have access to the policy. All practitioners know who the named person with lead responsibility for safeguarding children is and what to do if the named person is unavailable.

Practitioners supervise children carefully and ensure they are always safeguarded. They know their children well and use their understanding effectively to prevent accidents.

All room practitioners have completed safeguarding children training.

Detailed records of the children are kept and confidentiality is maintained.

From good to better

All safeguarding children policies and procedures are in place. All practitioners are consulted when policies are being renewed. Efficient recruitment and vetting procedures take place to ensure all adults are suitable to work with or to be in regular contact with children. All practitioners have access to the policy. They know who the named person with lead responsibility for safeguarding children is and what to do if the named person is unavailable.

Practitioners understand that the safeguarding of children is of supreme importance. They would not hesitate to take the difficult step of acting on a concern. They know when and how to seek advice, and they report concerns competently to the appropriate people and authorities.

All practitioners, including domestic and administrative, recently completed training in safeguarding children, to ensure that the children are extremely well protected in the long term.

Full records are kept on all children. These are stored securely and confidentially. In the event of an accident parents are contacted at the earliest opportunity, and they sign a record to confirm that they have been told about the accident.

Enjoy and Achieve

Audit

	Outstanding	Good	Satisfactory	Inadequate 1	Inadequate 2
Children's individual needs are met and their welfare is promoted	Superb partnership between practitioners, parents and external agencies to work together to meet each child's needs. Children have a clear understanding of their own needs and a mature respect for the needs of others.	Good partnership between practitioners, parents and external agencies to work together to meet each child's needs. Children understand their own needs and begin to respect the needs of others.	Practitioners, parents and external agencies work sufficiently well together to meet each child's needs. Children begin to understand their own needs, and with adult support, become aware of the needs of others.	Parents, practitioners and external agencies do not work sufficiently well together to meet each child's needs. Children show little regard of the needs of others in the setting.	Parents, practitioners and external agencies do not work together to meet each child's needs. Children show a disregard for the needs of others in the setting.
EYFS actively promoted and implemented	A rich homely environment with an exciting range of sensory experiences offered. Practitioners follow children's interests and develop the environment and their planning accordingly. Opportunity to move freely indoors and out.	A homely environment, with a wide range of sensory experiences offered. Practitioners follow children's interests and develop some aspects of the environment in response to children. Opportunity to move freely outdoors.	Some aspects of a homely environment. Some sensory experiences available all the time. Others planned for. Some evidence of environment being developed in response to children's interests. Regular opportunities to play outdoors but planned by adults.	Few aspects of a homely environment with limited sensory experiences. Little evidence of environment and experiences being developed in response to children's needs. Few opportunities for outdoor play.	No aspects of homely features in environment. Few sensory experiences available. No evidence of development of environment in response to children's interests. No opportunities for outdoor play.
Children's attitudes to learning	Children are animated and enthusiastic and make choices independently about their activities. Behaviour is of a consistently high standard. Children show high levels of curiosity, imagination and concentration.	Children are confident and have a positive attitude to learning. Children are involved, motivated and engaged in a broad range of activities. Behaviour is of a good standard. They show good levels of independence, curiosity, imagination and concentration.	Children are sufficiently confident to independently make choices. They show interest in a range of activities. Behaviour is satisfactory. They have satisfactory levels of independence, curiosity, imagination and concentration and use all their senses to explore.	Children have limited confidence and self-assurance. Children need adult support to play. Children show little interest in limited activities. Children follow adult directives. Behaviour is sometimes poor. Curiosity and imagination is limited.	Children have little confidence and cannot play effectively even with adult support. Children unresponsive, bored and show scant interest in activities. Behaviour is unacceptable. Children have under developed sense of curiosity and imagination and ability to concentrate.

	Outstanding	Good	Satisfactory	Inadequate 1	Inadequate 2
Quality of teaching	Teaching is dynamic, inspiring and challenging. Activities and experiences are rich, varied and imaginative and well matched to children's needs and interests. Practitioners have expert knowledge of the EYFS, varied and exciting teaching methods and a full understanding of how children learn and progress.	Teaching provides realistic challenge. Practitioners understand children's needs and provide a wide range of activities and experiences to move them on. Teaching is rooted in a secure knowledge of the EYFS, a good range of teaching methods and knowledge of how children learn and progress.	Teaching is appropriate for all groups of children. Practitioners understand children's needs and provide a sufficient range of activities and experiences. They have a sound knowledge of the EYFS, a reasonable range of teaching methods and some understanding of how children learn and progress.	Teaching is ineffective. There is little to capture children's interests and activities are not matched to children's needs Practitioners have an incomplete knowledge of the EYFS. They are insecure in their understanding of how children learn and have limited teaching methods. Time and resources are not used effectively.	Teaching is poor. Range of activities is too narrow to cover the areas of learning. Practitioners do not take into account children's needs and interests in their plans. They have low expectations of children, offer little challenge and have a weak knowledge of the EYFS. Teaching methods are inappropriate and fail to engage children.
Quality of Learning	Children are engrossed in an exciting range of purposeful and developmentally appropriate indoor and outdoor activities, which provide high levels of challenge appropriate to their age and stage. Children make rapid progress towards Early Learning Goals.	Children are engaged in a broad range of developmentally appropriate indoor and outdoor activities, which provide good levels of challenge. They are keen to offer their own ideas and respond well to challenges. Overall, children make sound progress towards the Early Learning Goals.	Children show interest in a range of purposeful, first hand activities and sometimes offer their own ideas, although these are not always sufficiently challenging to help children to take the next step. Overall, children make some progress towards the Early Learning Goals.	Children have little interest in limited activities. Learning is repetitive and lacks challenge. There is insufficient adult attention to help them progress. An overly adult-directed environment. Children are often left to their own devices. Children make insufficient progress towards the Early Learning Goals.	Children show scant interest in few activities. There is no evidence of learning. They receive no adult attention. All activities adult-initiated. Children always left to their own devices. Children make no progress towards the Early Learning Goals.
Assessment and record keeping	Observation and assessment is rigorous and the information gained used very effectively to inform next steps of learning. Continual and rigorous monitoring and evaluation of observations and assessment procedures are in place. Excellent children's profiles are evident giving a clear picture of progress.	Observation and assessment is thorough and the information gained used effectively to inform next steps of learning. Observation and assessment procedures are monitored and evaluated. Individual children's profiles are developing well and show children's progress.	Observations and assessment and the use of information gained from it are satisfactory, but sometimes inconsistent and not used sufficiently to inform next steps of learning. Individual children's profiles are beginning to be developed and some show children's progress.	Observations and assessment is inadequate. The information gathered is inappropriate and not used to inform next steps of learning. Assessment and record keeping is rarely monitored and evaluated. Some evidence of children's profiles but sufficient progress not illustrated.	Assessment is unsatisfactory. No evidence of observations of children. Practitioners fail to observe and assess children's progress. No evidence of children's profiles. No records of children's progress.

What will happen during the Ofsted inspection?

What will the inspector expect to see?	What might the inspector ask?	What can I do to prepare?
• Children involved in a broad range of activities, which support their language and mathematical thinking and imagination • Positive relationships demonstrated between practitioners, children and parents	• How do you ensure your provision meets the needs of all children that attend? • Could you explain your settling in procedure? • Do you have a key worker system? Can you explain how this works?	• Ensure that your planning is inclusive for all children • Ensure their individual records are up to date • Make sure the key worker is aware of their role and responsibility
• A rich, homely environment • Children moving freely indoors and outdoors	• How is the EYFS Framework used to plan for 0–5 year olds?	• Ensure all practitioners have knowledge of the EYFS 0–5 Framework • Ensure there is evidence of how the framework influences the outcomes for children in each room
• Children playing and learning as they choose from a range of activities • Adults responding to children's interests • Adults praising and encouraging children, thus promoting positive behaviour • Activities available for both active play and relaxation	• Tell me about the choice you offer children and how is this monitored? • Are children involved in the planning of activities? • Where can children relax/sleep if they wish to?	• Ensure any observations are recorded and practitioners encourage children to reach their milestones • Ensure each room has identified areas for rest/sleep i.e. beanbags, cushions
• Children and parents individually welcomed into the setting • Displays that reflect the local community and where the children live	• If a child attends a school how do you ensure that information is shared with all parties? • How do you keep up to date with local events?	• Review communication strategy with local schools and parents • Collate local information, newsletters for reference

Policies and documentation

Policies

- Involving and consulting with children
- Anti-bullying policy
- Equipment and resources
- Excursions
- Behaviour management
- SEN
- Equal opportunities
- Working in partnership with parents
- Care, learning and play

Documentation

- Children's registration documents
- Individual care plans and IEPs
- Activity planning
- Assessments and observation records

Other resources

- Children's profiles
- Photographs of children and their work

Examples of good practice

Children's individual needs are met and their welfare is promoted

Examples of good practice

Room staff meetings are held with a planned agenda. Sometimes, staff meeting time is given over to training. Parent's evenings are held once a term and parents receive a termly newsletter including nursery news and events. There is an information board for parents, which displays statutory information, curriculum and general news. Daily discussions are held with parents about events and outings. The manager meets with parents when a child is due to start at the setting and information is gathered about the child. The parent is provided with a brochure/welcome booklet.

The setting embraces support from outside agencies. There are close links with the school setting and information about individual children is shared. An outreach support worker is engaged with a baby in the sensory area within the baby room. The outreach worker has a good relationship with other practitioners in the room.

Two children are visiting the room they are soon to move into, to make transition smoother.

Children have respect for other children's needs. A group of children are engaged in a discussion with a practitioner about moving their noisy activity away from a sleeping child. A child falls over and is comforted by another child who is praised by the practitioner.

From good to better

Weekly meetings are held where possible to discuss individual children and to plan. Regular practitioner in-house training takes place. Parents receive a monthly newsletter with current news and advance notice of future holiday activities and events. Daily diaries are kept about the children and discussed with the parents. The parents' noticeboard displays photographs and articles relating to the Early Years Foundation Stage and current early years practice.

There is a good relationship with outside agencies. The room leader is in attendance at a review meeting of a child with additional needs who attends both settings.

There is an effective transition programme in place. A practitioner visits the room with a child that is soon to move into. Practitioners share information about the child and work hard to help him feel welcome in his environment. The children who are soon to start in the school nursery make visits there.

Children are sensitive to each other's needs.

Examples of good practice
EYFS actively promoted and implemented

Examples of good practice

Most rooms are homely. They have practitioners feeding babies and reading stories sitting on cosy sofas. A little boy is looking at a book sitting on the sofa. There are attractive textured rugs and cushions placed on the floor adding definition and interest to the environment. Exciting treasure baskets of everyday objects are being investigated by a baby independently while a practitioner responds with encouraging smiles. A child is exploring cooked pasta on a builder's tray with bare toes. Photos of children exploring gloop, jelly, glue and paint are displayed at child height. A song on the CD player excites a two year old and the practitioner acknowledges this and introduces instruments and other songs. Children are jumping excitedly in puddles outside and some are digging in the soil.

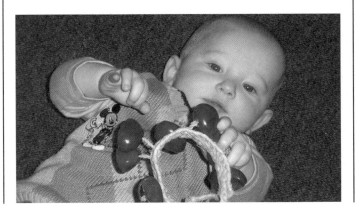

From good to better

All rooms are homely with sofas, comfy chairs, drapes and hanging voiles where appropriate. Interesting everyday objects hang from mobiles adding interest for children. Children are engaged in domestic activities. A group of children are baking with a practitioner. Children are outside washing baby clothes in soapy water and hanging them on a low level washing line. A group of children are engaged in sand and water activities and are encouraged by a practitioner to respond to open ended questions e.g. 'What will happen if you put the sponge in the water?' and 'What does the coral feel like?'

Children have the opportunity to move freely indoors and out. Some children are in the garden collecting autumn leaves for an activity.

Examples of good practice
Children's attitudes to learning

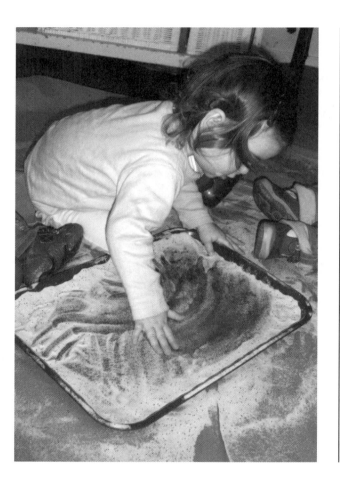

Examples of good practice

Children are happy and settled and enjoy themselves supported by caring adults. Children are confident in initiating their own learning; they are excited by the activities provided. Two boys are excited by construction materials and begin to build a tower for *Spiderman* to climb.

The children are calm and relaxed which helps them to make good progress towards their personal, social and emotional development. The children are polite and considerate towards each other, which the practitioner acknowledges with praise. They are learning to share favourite toys. Their behaviour is very good and they enjoy their independence by helping themselves to snacks and drinks.

The children are keen to participate in all activities and select tasks independently. They are confident to make decisions, explore and investigate and relate well to others. They understand, for example, that spiders spin webs to catch their own food.

From good to better

Children enter the nursery with enthusiasm and excitement and are eager to play with each other. They confidently engage in the challenging environment. A dinosaur environment captures the attention of a child who quickly identifies a Tyrannosaurus Rex and proudly tells his key person its name. The practitioner responds by asking the child what he thinks it would eat. The child informed her that it uses its long neck to eat leaves from the trees.

Children look for answers, make decisions and solve problems. They take part in experiments, for example, finding out what will sink or float by using the conker they found in the garden and the pumpkin they grew in the vegetable garden.

Behaviour is excellent. Children are persistent and have high levels of concentration. A child fetches writing materials and scissors, makes a picture, cuts it out, writes her name on it and then hangs it up to dry on a washing line with pegs. She clears away afterwards and goes off happily.

Examples of good practice
Quality of teaching

Examples of good practice

A good range of stimulating, practical activities is provided. Practitioners provide a calm environment and value the children. They help them feel good about themselves by frequently providing positive support, praise and encouragement. Children benefit from a range of activities outside the setting. They go for walks to the shops, to the park to feed the ducks or they go out for a picnic. Practitioners plan these activities well and use them as effective opportunities to help children's learning.

Practitioners give children time to develop their ideas and interests, enabling them to expand their knowledge and understanding of the world in which they live. Children explore a wealth of living things from plants and trees in the woods to snails, worms and frogs in the pond.

Practitioners plan effectively from the EYFS Framework to involve children and further their development.

Practitioners make good use of questioning as they challenge children to recognise and compare colour, number, shape and size to support learning. Practitioners are particularly receptive to the quieter children and encourage them to be involved in play. Practitioners achieve a balance between supervised activities and allowing children to create from their imagination, e.g. singing and dancing.

From good to better

Practitioners understand how children learn and develop and know how to engage their interest, ensuring that activities are attractive, developmentally appropriate and challenging. The children choose from a wide variety of materials to mark make including fluorescent labels, speech bubble shapes, book formats and a variety of greeting card shapes. Practitioners are involved with children as they play, knowing how to engage them in discussion by asking open ended questions e.g. 'I wonder why...?' 'I wonder what happens when...?' and waiting for children to think about their reply.

Practitioners make full use of the indoor and outdoor environment to maximise opportunities for children's progress and enjoyment. Drapes are hung from trees and fences outside to create dens. An outdoor shed is developed into a fire station and vehicles become fire engines. The children have developed appropriate signs. Practitioners are able to adapt activities in response to children's individual needs and spontaneously take advantage of everyday experiences. Children feel the effects of the wind on their skin or pretend to be a leaf whirling around. Practitioners join in enthusiastically with these activities extending children's understanding and helping them to express themselves creatively.

Examples of good practice
Quality of learning

Examples of good practice

Children are involved in stimulating practical experiences that allow them to learn new skills and to talk and listen. During a baking activity, the practitioner discusses numbers and textures and the child responds with confidence asking many questions, and clearly learning from the experience.

Children respond excitedly to a wide range of creative activities. They sing and dance with gusto, love role play and explore with paint and other materials.

The practitioners guide children to discuss their own or others creative ideas and encourage the children to observe and express their thoughts and develop their language.

Practitioners offer the children challenges by providing open-ended resources to enhance their learning.

Evidence of progression towards the Early Learning Goals can be seen as observations and individual planning in children's profiles.

From good to better

Dynamic and motivated practitioners play with the children and offer experiences that are based on the children's individual interests, needs and abilities. Through these experiences children are encouraged by highly skilled and enthusiastic practitioners to take the next step and who help them to see ways to extend their play, allowing the children to grow in confidence and to keep them focused. Outside they play imaginatively and use the apparatus as castles, airplanes or space rockets. A group of children have connected pieces of guttering together to create a waterway from the water tray, to a builder's tray on the ground nearby.

Practitioners question and respond to children's ideas about their play and regularly gather photographic and observational evidence from all areas of learning and development.

Examples of good practice
Assessment and record keeping

Examples of good practice

Spontaneous observations are made on individual children on a daily basis. Group observations are planned for focussed activities. The observations are used to plan for next steps for individual children. Practitioners evaluate their practice through their observations and planning, and develop the environment accordingly.

All children have their own personal profile that contains information about the child. Photographs and evidence is referenced to the EYFS Framework.

From good to better

Spontaneous observations are made when children demonstrate significant progress on a daily basis. A note was made of a child successfully pulling himself up on the sofa for the first time. Planned focussed activities are carried out and observations are recorded. Practitioners discuss the observations and use the information to plan next steps for learning.

All children have their own personal profile that contains relevant observations, photographs of the child's experiences and any relevant documentation, e.g. an IEP, medical history. The profiles indicate clearly that the child is making good progress through relevant photographs with statements clearly referenced to the areas of learning and development.

Make a Positive Contribution

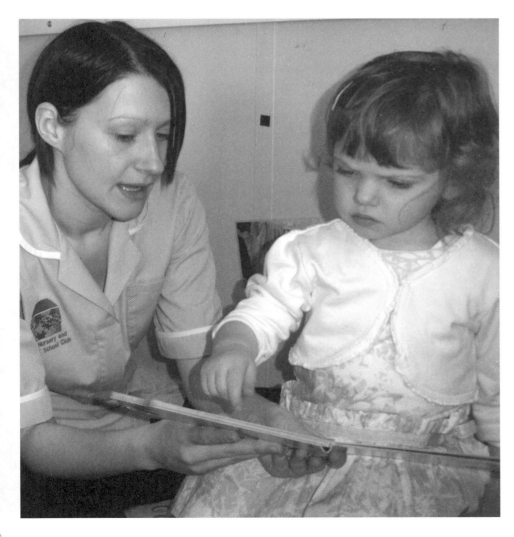

Audit

	Outstanding	Good	Satisfactory	Inadequate 1	Inadequate 2
Practitioners promote equal opportunity and anti-discriminatory practice for all children	Resources reflect positive images of culture, ethnicity, gender and disability. All practitioners ensure the environment allows for all children to take part. All practitioners have clear expectations of children's behaviour according to age and stage. Information collected on the children is detailed and thorough.	Most resources reflect positive images of culture, ethnicity, gender and disability. The environment allows for children to be included and involved. Most practitioners have clear expectations of children's behaviour according to age and stage. Information collected on the children is thorough.	Some resources reflect positive images of culture, ethnicity, gender and disability. Most practitioners ensure the environment allows for all children to take part. Practitioners generally manage children and their behaviour appropriately. Information on the children is adequate.	Few resources reflect the background of many children and the wider community. Some evidence of the environment being adapted to include all children. Practitioners are uncertain about effective ways of managing children and their behaviour. Information collected on the children is inconsistent.	Little or no resources to reflect the background of the children and the wider community. Little or no evidence of the environment being adapted to include all children Practitioners are unable to manage children well and have unclear expectations of their behaviour. Little or no evidence of information on the children.
Welfare and development of children with special needs are promoted	All practitioners are confident in their knowledge of child development and very effective procedures are in place for the identification of children with special needs. The environment is very effective and meets the needs of all children. Practitioners are confident in keeping observational records. All practitioners have positive attitudes towards the care of the children and act as excellent role models. Very strict confidentialities are adhered to.	Practitioners have sound knowledge and understanding of how to identify children with special needs and have procedures in place. The environment meets the developmental needs of children. Practitioners keep observational records. Practitioners act as good role models and promote positive attitudes with the children. Confidentialities are respected.	Appropriate procedures are in place for the identification of children with special needs. The environment is appropriately organised to meet the needs of children. Practitioners keep appropriate observational records. Most practitioners promote positive attitudes with the children. Confidentialities are kept.	Practitioners are not always consistent in their knowledge of child development and have ineffective procedures in place to identify children with special needs. The environment is not appropriately organised to include all children. Little evidence of regular observations being made. Few practitioners promote positive attitudes with the children. Confidentialities not always adhered to.	Practitioners have little knowledge of child development and do not have procedures in place to identify children with special needs. The environment is inappropriate for inclusive practice. No evidence of written observations. Practitioners do not act as good role models and do not promote positive attitudes with the children. Little or no regard paid to confidentialities.

	Outstanding	Good	Satisfactory	Inadequate 1	Inadequate 2
Children's behaviour is managed in a way which promotes their welfare and development	All practitioners are friendly, calm and have consistently high expectations of children's behaviour. All practitioners exhibit excellent behaviour management techniques. They act as excellent role models. Children know what is expected of them and are exceptionally well behaved. Parents are fully involved in reaching decisions about their child.	Practitioners are cheerful, confident and consistent in their use of praise and encouragement. Practitioners manage children and their behaviour well. They act as effective role models. Children show a good understanding of how to behave. Parents are consulted on all decisions about their child.	Practitioners are pleasant and encourage children to understand responsible behaviour. Children are generally well behaved. They are settled and happy and make positive relationships with adults and peers. Parents are kept informed of their child's development.	Practitioners show little interest in children and give them little attention. Children's behaviour is poor and disruptive and little guidance is given to children to manage their own behaviour. Children are mainly left to their own devices. Parents are not always kept informed of their child's development.	Practitioners are disinterested and disengaged. Children's behaviour is poor and disruptive and children show little understanding of behavioural boundaries and fail to learn how to manage their own behaviour. Parents are not kept informed of their child's development.
Work in partnership with parents to meet the needs of the children	Excellent communication with parents. All practitioners are welcoming and share information daily. Parents contribute to, and support, their child's learning. The setting is promoted in the community and visitors are invited in regularly. Outings are organised within the local community. Displays reflect the local community and society in which we live in an imaginative and exciting way.	Effective communication with the parents. All practitioners are friendly and share information regularly. Parents give information in exchange and show some interest in supporting their child's learning. The setting is promoted in the community and visitors are invited in when appropriate. Displays reflect the community and society in an interesting way.	Inconsistent communication with parents. Some practitioners are friendly and sometimes share information. Some parents share information and show some interest in supporting their child's learning. The setting is promoted in the community and visitors are invited in occasionally. Generally displays reflect the community and society.	Little communication with parents. Practitioners do not promote a welcoming environment. Information shared irregularly. Parents are not encouraged to support their child's learning. The setting is sometimes promoted in the community. Visitors are rarely invited in. Displays do not reflect the community and society.	No communication with parents. Setting not warm and welcoming. No information shared with parents. The setting is not promoted in the community and visitors are never invited in. No displays reflecting the community or society.

What will happen during the Ofsted inspection?

What will the inspector expect to see?	What might the inspector ask?	What can I do to prepare?
• Inclusive practice demonstrated • Resources that reflect positive images of culture, ethnicity, gender and disability • The physical environment is adapted to allow children to take part in activities alongside their peers • Good behaviour being valued and encouraged according to the children's different stages of development	• What do you understand by the meaning of inclusive practice? • How do you identify the need to adapt the environment? • Explain your behaviour management policy? • When would you implement restraint?	• Ensure practitioners access training where possible • Review equipment and resources regularly
• Detailed and effective individual children's records	• How would you liaise with parents or other agencies if you had a concern regarding a child? • Where would this be recorded?	• Ensure children's records are up to date
• Practitioners with clear boundaries when dealing with challenging behaviour • Practitioners explaining and reasoning with children when behaviour is not acceptable	• Explain your behaviour management procedure? • How do you inform parents of behaviour issues? • What procedures do you have to monitor consistent behaviour issues?	• Discuss and review the behaviour management policy and procedures and consult with staff on their views • Ensure all staff access behaviour management training
• All children and parents are welcomed daily • Displays reflecting local community information and the society in which the children live in	• How are you informed of local events and activities?	• Collating local information to inform practitioners and parents of forthcoming activities

Policies and documentation

Policies

- Equal opportunities
- Working in partnership with parents
- Excursions
- Involving and consulting with children
- SEN
- Behaviour management
- Students and volunteers
- Confidentiality policy

Documentation

- Complaints procedure
- Children's records, care plans and IEPs
- Written agreements with parents
- SEN Code of Practice
- SENCO Training Certificates
- Assessment and observation records

Other resources

- Parental agreements with regard to how they wish their child to be cared for
- A private but homely space to talk to parents

Examples of good practice

Practitioners promote equal opportunities and anti-discriminatory practice for all children

Examples of good practice

Practitioners display photographs of families of different cultures and provide interest tables and displays celebrating festivals. There is a wide range of resources reflecting all cultures.

Practitioners encourage children to bring in photos of family and friends and offer resources and activities to include all children including those with disabilities and SEN.

Practitioners consider and plan the environment and ensure all children can participate. Practitioners keep accurate records on individual children and share information with parents and other practitioners when necessary.

From good to better

Practitioners encourage children to bring photographs and artefacts from home and are involved in activities to celebrate a range of festivals including food tasting and dressing up e.g. parent invited into setting wearing traditional dress. Regular meetings are arranged with parents and external agencies to update and review children's progress with regard to behaviour issues and SEN.

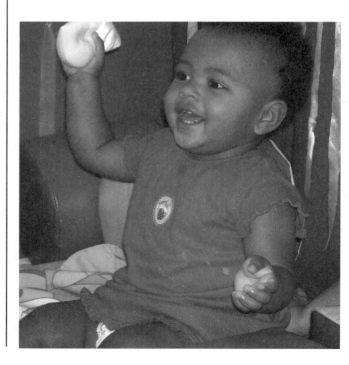

Examples of good practice
Welfare and development of children with special needs is promoted

Examples of good practice

All practitioners access special needs awareness training and are aware of special needs policies and procedures. Practitioners are able to refer concerns about children to the setting's SENCO or childminder SENCO e.g. a practitioner notices that a baby of ten months is not attempting to sit up yet.

Practitioners offer resources that are age and stage appropriate for all children and incorporate the EYFS when considering the environment e.g. different rugs/textures on the floor when babies are crawling.

Practitioners observe children and keep a record of these observations including photographs of their experiences.

Practitioners interact with the children using praise and good manners e.g. saying 'please' and 'thank you' at meal times.

Practitioners understand the procedures regarding confidentiality and that records and information about children must be securely stored but accessible.

From good to better

All practitioners have attended EYFS training. Additional needs training is in place from outside agencies such as Speech and Language Services who would deliver training in the setting.

Through observations practitioners can recognise when the environment needs adapting or changing to follow children's interests and offer stimulating challenging experiences to plan for the children's next steps e.g. a practitioner notices that resources are not being used and need to be changed or a new experience offered.

Practitioners consistently show respect for each other, parents and children. Practitioners speak politely and use appropriate language and take an interest in the children at all times e.g. thanking a parent, practitioner or visitor for holding open the door or welcoming a child back to the setting after being on holiday or being ill.

Practitioners understand and recognise the need for confidentiality and provision is made for private consultations with each other, external agencies and parents e.g. parents invited to multi-disciplinary meeting in private room within the setting, or at another venue if this is preferred.

Examples of good practice
Children's behaviour is managed in a way which promotes their welfare and development

Examples of good practice

Children are welcomed into the setting and practitioners demonstrate effective role modelling when greeting and saying goodbye to parents, e.g. smiling, and offering comments to the child.

Practitioners use appropriate behaviour management techniques in recognising a child's frustration and intervening before conflict occurs e.g. using distraction techniques before a child knocks over another child's model. Practitioners implement behaviour management and offer positive routines to encourage appropriate behaviour.

Practitioners have good relationships with parents/carers and are informed every day about decisions regarding their children e.g. a practitioner will discuss with the parent what their child had for lunch, how long they slept for and what activities they were involved in.

From good to better

Children are individually welcomed into the setting e.g. smiling, gesturing, and complimenting children while encouraging them to hang up their coats and bags and praising them when they do so. The children acknowledge that positive behaviour will be rewarded e.g. praise for helping another child find a favourite toy.

Practitioners remain calm and utterly composed when they explain, at the child's level, why certain actions are unacceptable e.g. fighting with other children. The children know that inappropriate behaviour is not acceptable. The consistent approach from all the practitioners enables children to understand the difference between right and wrong.

Parents are encouraged to contribute towards their child's learning and development and excellent methods of communication are in place.

Examples of good practice

Work in partnership with parents to meet the needs of the children

Examples of good practice

Practitioners communicate well with parents and share pertinent information with them about the activities within the setting. Parents are welcome at all times within the setting. The parents are encouraged to share information with practitioners about likes, dislikes, favourite toys and books etc.

Parents are interested in the experiences the children are offered and the progress they are making. They are encouraged where possible to join the children on specific outings and activities. The children visit the local library and sometimes parents will be invited in e.g. to bath a new baby or to bake. There is a parent's noticeboard, which displays information about the setting and the practitioners working there.

From good to better

Practitioners communicate extremely well with parents and share individual information with them every day. There is a friendly trust and a bond between practitioners and parents, which allows the parents to share information with confidence.

Parents are encouraged to participate in their child's learning. They contribute verbally within the setting and continue to support the child at home e.g. daily record books, collecting things for displays or treasure baskets that will be used in the setting.

The practitioners are involved in community events and make links with other settings e.g. storytelling sessions at the local library and events throughout the year at the local Children's Centre. Parents are kept informed of local events on their noticeboard where they can also take leaflets relating to childcare e.g. sleep patterns, healthy eating and toilet training. The noticeboard for parents is informative and displayed imaginatively with details about opening times, routines, policies and procedures and forthcoming events locally and within the setting. Space is available for private discussions with parents.

Organisation to promote Good Outcomes for Children

Audit

	Outstanding	Good	Satisfactory	Inadequate 1	Inadequate 2
Practitioners caring for children are suitable	There is a high percentage of qualified level 2 and 3 practitioners. All practitioners working towards level 3. Extensive and robust recruitment and vetting procedures are in place.	Qualified practitioners are above the minimum 50% level 2 with a proportion at level 3 and some working towards level 3. Sound recruitment and vetting procedures are in place.	50% of practitioners are level 2 qualified. All practitioners are appropriately vetted and checks carried out.	Inadequately qualified practitioners on duty i.e. below 50% at level 2. Not all practitioner checks have been carried out posing a risk to children.	No qualified practitioners at all. No relevant checks carried out putting children at risk.
Adult-child ratios are maintained. Training and qualification requirements are met.	An excellent child to practitioner ratio is maintained at all times. Extensive systems on practitioner and child attendance are maintained and monitored. Practitioners are deployed and organised effectively, with good lines of communication between them. Practitioners are valued and their ongoing professional development is promoted and supported. All relevant training and qualifications requirements are exceeded.	Above a minimum of two practitioners on duty at all times. Effective practitioner and child registers in place. Practitioners are organised effectively. However, there is inconsistent communication between practitioners. Practitioners are given opportunities for professional development with support. Relevant training and qualifications are above the minimum requirements.	Minimum staffing ratios maintained but are inconsistent. Practitioner and child registers kept. Practitioners not organised effectively with some communication between them. Some opportunities for professional development are offered. Minimum requirements for qualifications and training are maintained.	Inadequate number of practitioners on duty some of the time. Ratios not adhered to. Registers not regularly maintained. Little evidence of practitioners' organisation and communication. Little professional development undertaken. Lack of support. Practitioners lack relevant specific training and qualifications.	Inadequate number of practitioners on duty at all times. No evidence of practitioner or child registration. Practitioners are inappropriately organised with no communication. No professional development undertaken and no support. Practitioners do not have the relevant specific training and qualifications.

	Outstanding	Good	Satisfactory	Inadequate 1	Inadequate 2
Space and resources are organised to meet the children's needs effectively	Space and resources are organised effectively to maximise play opportunities for children ensuring their needs are met.	Space and resources are well planned and consideration is given to meeting children's needs.	Space and resources are organised with some consideration given to meeting children's needs.	Space and resources are organised ineffectively and little consideration is given to meeting children's needs.	No evidence of organisation of space and resources. Children's needs are not met.
Required records, policies and procedures that promote the welfare, care and learning of children are maintained	Ofsted are notified immediately of all relevant changes and detailed evidence is kept. All detailed records, polices and procedures are in place, reviewed and maintained regularly and stored securely, if appropriate.	Ofsted are notified as soon as possible of all relevant changes and evidence is kept. Most detailed records, policies and procedures are in place and reviewed and maintained effectively and stored securely, if appropriate.	Ofsted are notified of all relevant changes. Some records, polices and procedures are in place and stored.	Ofsted are not always notified of all relevant changes. Few records, polices and procedures are in place.	Ofsted are never notified of any relevant changes. No records, polices or procedures in place.
Leadership and management	The manager is dynamic and inspirational and has a clear vision for the overall management and development of the setting. Excellent communication between management and practitioners ensures strong effective relationships.	The manager is effective and has a clear vision for the overall management of the setting. Strong communication between management and practitioners ensures effective relationships.	The manager is sometimes effective but has a limited vision for the overall management of the setting. Communication between management and practitioners ensures appropriate relationships.	The manager is ineffective and the overall management of the setting is inconsistent. Little communication between management and practitioners resulting in ineffective relationships.	The manager is ineffective and the overall management of the setting is poor. No communication between management and practitioners resulting in poor relationships.

What will happen during the Ofsted inspection?

What will the inspector expect to see?	What might the inspector ask?	What can I do to prepare?
• Detailed personal records including training • Appropriate recruitment procedures • Recommended qualified staffing levels maintained	• Explain how the recruitment was carried out? • Can you tell me the adult to child ratio for each age group?	• Ensure all personal files are up to date
• Accurate practitioners rotas and children's daily registers • Up-to-date training and professional development records	• What would happen if a practitioner was unable to come into work or a childminder was ill? • How do you identify training needs?	• Prepare a contingency plan in the event of practitioner absence • Ensure all practitioners have access to the Early Years Training Directory
• Practitioners making good use of space and resources so that children are well cared for and supported while they are in the setting • Some adults working directly with the children • Some children engaged independently in a task	• Is there a budget for buying and replacing resources? • Are practitioners able to choose specific resources for their room? • What would you do if a child needed one to one care?	• In-house audit of equipment and resources
• Ofsted have been informed of all current and past changes and events. • Records accessible and stored securely and confidentiality is maintained • Up-to-date, accessible policies and procedures available for inspection and to parents	• How do you ensure Ofsted are informed of changes to the setting? • Can you explain the meaning of confidentiality? • Explain how your policies and procedures are reviewed and who is involved in this process?	• Keep copies of Significant Changes Form • Discuss confidentiality in a staff meeting • Revisit all policies and procedures, check dates and practitioners knowledge of these
• Evidence that the manager or childminder has undertaken/is undertaking an Early Years qualification • Evidence of effective staff communication through regular staff meetings and one to one supervision	• Can you identify your own strengths and weaknesses since undertaking this qualification? • Are practitioners able to contribute to their supervision? • Are practitioners able to contribute to the staff meeting agenda?	• Complete a SWOT analysis • Ask practitioners to come up with agenda items for staff meetings

Policies and documentation

Policies

- Selection and recruitment
- Induction
- Students and volunteers
- Staffing policies
- Smoking, alcohol and drugs
- Staff development and training
- SEN
- Uncollected child
- Lost child
- Complaints
- Confidentiality
- Equipment and resources
- Admissions
- Working in partnership with parents
- Arrivals and departures

Documentation

- Business plan
- Contingency plan
- Operational plan
- Staff rotas
- Staff induction packs
- Children's registers
- Visitor's book
- Training certificates
- Significant changes documentation
- Staff personnel information
- Staff meeting agendas and minutes

Other resources

- Staff signing in and out register
- SWOT analysis

Examples of good practice
Practitioners caring for children are suitable to do so

Examples of good practice

Qualifications are above minimum 50% level 2 with most practitioners working towards a level 3 qualification. All practitioners are given training information and are encouraged to attend. There are procedures in place for the recruitment of staff to ensure the safety of all children e.g. all applicants are required to show proof of ID, qualification certificates and undergo a CRB check. Childminders ensure that all adults, 16 years and over, living within the home have undertaken a CRB check.

From good to better

The manager is working towards an HE qualification and all staff are working towards a level 3 qualification.

The manager is proactive in ensuring that all practitioners have access to relevant training and promotes self-development and vetting via training directory, college literature and training agency information.

There are consistent procedures in place for the recruitment of staff to ensure the safety of all children, e.g. all applicants are required to show proof of ID, qualification certificate and undergo a CRB check. Photocopies of all information are taken and checked.

Childminders ensure that all adults, 16 years and over, living within the home have undertaken a CRB check, that this information is recorded and that they have informed Ofsted of these changes. The childminder is working towards a relevant level 3 qualification.

Examples of good practice
Adult/child ratios are maintained. Training and qualification requirements are met

Examples of good practice

There is always a minimum of two practitioners on duty at the beginning of the day and in each room at all times. Practitioners ensure that child registers are completed on a daily basis. Practitioners are allocated time to ensure this is done. Practitioner rotas are maintained and updated daily. Practitioners are informed of any changes. Practitioners are required to sign in and out using a staff register.

Practitioners are signposted to relevant training information, supported and encouraged to attend. Childminders ensure that all relevant qualifications are up to date.

From good to better

The setting maintains a high standard of adult supervision and has above the minimum ratio of two practitioners on duty during lunch times and at the beginning and end of the day. Child registers are completed and monitored on a daily basis by practitioners. There is a nominated person responsible for this duty. The manager ensures that all practitioners are informed daily of changes to the rota prior to the start of the day e.g. the manager carries out a walk around the nursery each morning to discuss changes for the day with all practitioners. There's a contingency plan in place should there be staff absence.

The manager is proactive in ensuring that all practitioners have access to relevant training and promotes self-development, through both external and internal training.

Childminders are proactive in ensuring that all qualifications remain valid at all times, i.e. booking on to courses in advance/prior to certification expiry dates and have a contingency plan with other registered childminders for everyday purposes.

Examples of good practice

Space and resources are organised to meet the children's needs effectively

Examples of good practice

Children have access to low level shelving and storage baskets. Baskets contain small amounts of equipment that can be clearly seen by the child. There is a wide variety of resources providing children with choices.

The childminder has arranged a specific area for messy play activities on a low level table, as the children are under three years old.

From good to better

Resources are regularly changed and adapted to ensure all children have variety and choice. Practitioners rearrange the environment to ensure large spaces around tables so that a child in a wheel chair can manoeuvre themselves freely around the room.

The childminder has a designated area for messy play activities.

Examples of good practice
Required records, policies and procedures that promote the welfare, care and learning of children are maintained

Examples of good practice

A Notification Form is completed and sent to Ofsted when there is a change or event at the setting e.g. there is a new manager or the childminder intends to/has moved house.

All appropriate policies and procedures are updated in consultation with some of the practitioners e.g. through senior team meetings. All appropriate policies and procedures are made available to practitioners and parents, either on display or in newsletters. Confidential records are kept in a locked cabinet/box.

From good to better

The setting maintains a file with all correspondence and notification changes to Ofsted. This contains a log of all contact with Ofsted.

All appropriate policies and procedures are updated and reviewed regularly in consultation with all practitioners and/or parents through meetings and questionnaires. Practitioner's views are valued by the setting's manager/proprietor, which enables policies and procedures to be adapted to enhance children's learning. The provider keeps up to date with wider issues in childcare, via the internet, that may impact on the welfare of children and therefore improve the policies and procedures. All relevant policies and procedures are given to all practitioners and parents on their induction with the setting.

Confidential records are kept in a locked cabinet in the manager's office. The office is also locked at the end of the day.

Examples of good practice
Leadership and management

Examples of good practice

The manager/childminder can identify their own strengths and weaknesses through a SWOT analysis and has been proactive in developing these areas through training and development. Practitioners record information for other practitioners in a daily diary.

Practitioners attend/organise social events that develop their partnership and team working, such as parents and practitioner summer fetes, firework parties and Christmas parties. There is a key worker system in place.

A childminder attends regular development training.

From good to better

The manager/childminder can identify their own and their colleagues strengths and weaknesses through all practitioners completing SWOT analysis prior to their supervision and has been proactive in addressing these areas through training and development.

The manager discusses her vision for the development of the setting in a staff meeting; practitioner's views are respected. Action plans are in place where appropriate.

There is a strong, well established team with excellent communication skills e.g. a practitioner/key worker going on holiday ensures that the practitioners in their room are fully aware of a new child starting while she is away, that they know the child's details, routines, additional needs and the parents' names. Practitioners attend team building training that develops their communication skills and team working.

The childminder is part of a childminding network that supports good practice and their own professional development.

Acknowledgements

This publication would not have been possible without the contributions from the following members of the Early Years Childcare Team:

Sue Marshall – Lead Officer
Judith Bridget – Advisory Teacher
Wendy Nixon – Early Years Foundation Stage Trainer
Lesley Granger – Childminder Development Coordinator
Joan Foy – Childcare Development Assistant
Liz Dixon – Childcare Development Assistant
Lynn McHugh – Quality and Training Officer
Tina Richardson – Toy Library Coordinator
Adele Cox – Outreach Inclusion/Support Coordinator
Peta Robinson – Outreach Inclusion Support Assistant

Additional support was kindly provided by:
Sally Featherstone, Educational Consultant

Abbreviations

COSHH	Control of Substances Hazardous to Health
CRB	Criminal Records Bureau
EYFS	Early Years Foundation Stage
HE	Higher Education
IEP	Individual Education Plan
LSB	Local Safeguarding Board
NQIN	National Quality Improvement Network
OFSTED	Office for Standards in Education
PAT	Portable Appliance Testing
RIDDOR	Reporting of Injuries, Diseases and Dangerous Occurrences Regulations
SEN	Special Educational Needs
SENCO	Special Educational Needs Coordinator
SWOT	Strengths Weaknesses Opportunities Threats